3/4/84

Body Noises

Body Noises

by Susan Kovacs Buxbaum
and Rita Golden Gelman

PICTURES BY ANGIE LLOYD

Alfred A. Knopf • New York

For Joel and Steve with love

THIS IS A BORZOI BOOK
PUBLISHED BY ALFRED A. KNOPF, INC.

Text Copyright © 1983 by S. & R. Gelman Associates, Inc. and
Susan Kovacs Buxbaum
Illustrations Copyright © 1983 by Angie Lloyd
All rights reserved under International and Pan-American
Copyright Conventions. Published in the United States by Alfred
A. Knopf, Inc., New York, and simultaneously in Canada by
Random House of Canada Limited, Toronto. Distributed by
Random House, Inc., New York. Manufactured in the United
States of America
2   4   6   8   0   9   7   5   3   1

Library of Congress Cataloging in Publication Data
Buxbaum, Susan Kovacs. Body noises.
Summary: Explains what causes body noises, such as snores,
yawns, sneezes, and sounds made by gas.
1. Body, Human—Juvenile literature.   2. Sounds—Juvenile
literature.   [1. Body, Human.   2. Sounds]
I. Gelman, Rita Golden.   II. Lloyd, Angie, ill.   III. Title.
QP37.B97   1983   612   83-320
ISBN 0-394-85771-2   ISBN 0-394-95771-7 (lib. bdg.)

ACKNOWLEDGMENTS

Thank you to the following people who patiently answered our endless questions:
Russell Crider, M.D., Vincent J. Fisher, M.D., Joseph B. Jacobs, M.D., Marshall Mundheim, M.D., Robert Raicht, M.D., and particularly Joel Buxbaum, M.D. And special thanks to Randi Klein for all her help.

CONTENTS

OOPS, EXCUSE ME

Everybody's body makes noises. Kings and queens burp. Parents and teachers hiccup. Movie stars and presidents expel gas. This book explains what causes body noises.

You will discover that some noises come from the way your body digests food. Other noises are signs that your body is taking care of minor problems like dust in your nose or something tickling your throat.

Most body noises are completely out of your control. You can't stop your burps, your snores, or your sneezes. You are not the boss of your hiccups, your coughs, or the weird grumbles that come from deep inside your body.

Sometimes your body warns you that it is about to make a noise. Then, if you want, you can leave the room. Other times there is absolutely nothing you can do except smile politely and say, "Oops, excuse me."

COUGHS

Something makes your throat feel funny. It might be a piece of dust. Or some food that went down your breathing tube by mistake. Or mucus that dripped down from your stuffed-up nose. You cough.

Sometimes you cough on purpose because you want to clear your throat. Other times you don't have any choice—you have to cough.

4

Coughs are useful. They clear your trachea, your main breathing tube, the same way you clear a straw when you blow through it.

If you have mucus or dust or food in your throat, a cough will help to clear it out. But if you have an infection, a cough won't make it go away. That's why, sometimes, you keep coughing. If you do a lot of coughing, your stomach and chest muscles might ache from all that extra exercise.

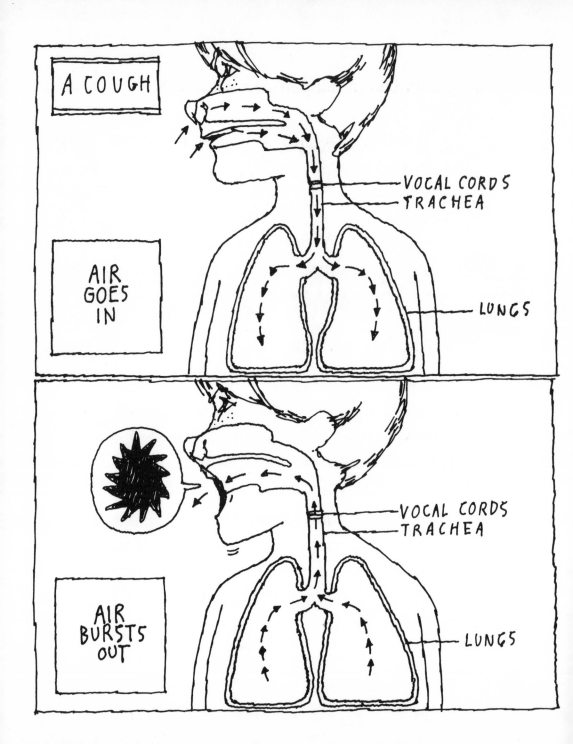

Every cough happens the same way:

1. You take a breath so that you have air in your lungs.

2. You close your throat and tighten up some of the muscles in your chest and abdomen, getting them ready for the big push.

3. Then the air bursts out.

Coughs make an exploding sound because the air that is pushed out of your lungs blasts its way through some closed flaps in the back of your throat. These flaps, called vocal cords, are forced open by the air, causing the explosion that we call a cough. They are the same vocal cords that make the noise when you sing or talk; you sound like you because of your vocal cords.

You can tell who is talking by the sound of a person's voice, but it's hard to tell who is coughing by the sound of the cough. People with high voices sometimes have low coughs. People with low voices sometimes have high coughs. That's because the sound of a cough depends upon how much air blasts out and whether or not the vocal cords are swollen from an infection.

SNEEZES

Sneezes are like coughs; they're just higher up. Coughs come from your throat, and even deeper down. Sneezes come from your nose. When something tickles or irritates your throat, you cough. When something tickles or irritates your nose, you sneeze.

In the first part of a sneeze, you suck in air through your vocal cords. That's the *aaaaaaah*. The *choo* part of a sneeze comes when the air blasts out through your mouth.

9

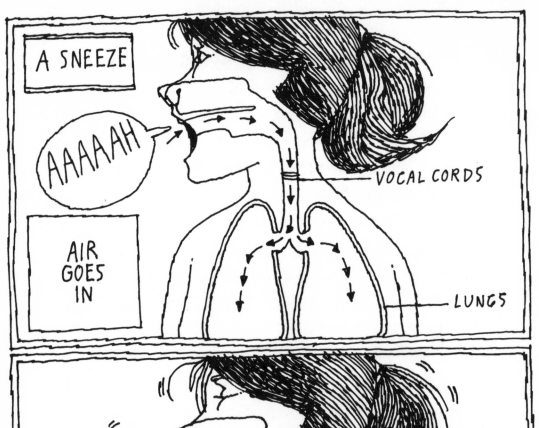

Sneezes can be very powerful. Scientists once measured the speed of a sneeze at more than one hundred miles an hour.

Sneezes happen when something is bothering the inside of your nose. Dust can make you sneeze. Smells can make you sneeze. Mucus from a stuffed-up nose can make you sneeze. Mucus can also make a sneeze very wet and messy. A sneeze is your body's way of getting rid of whatever is bothering your nose.

Different people sneeze in different ways.

Some sneeze through their noses. Some sneeze through their mouths.

There are noisy sneezers. And quiet, delicate sneezers.

There are sneezers who sneeze only once. And many who always sneeze twice. And others who sneeze many times in a row.

Doctors don't have any explanation for sneezing styles. "Probably habit," they say.

Years ago, people used to think that when a person sneezed, she or he was in some kind of danger. That's why saying "God bless you" got started.

In seventeenth-century Europe, people thought sneezes cleared people's minds and made them smart. The more people sneezed, the more important they were supposed to be. A truly important person, it was thought, could sneeze whenever she or he wanted to.

SNORES

People snore when they sleep, but only if they breathe through their mouths. Snores are noises that are made when parts of you inside your mouth and throat wiggle and flop as the air goes in and out.

All sorts of soft parts of you are involved in a snore. Tonsils are soft and floppy. So is your uvula, the flap that hangs down in the middle of your throat. Way in the back of your

14

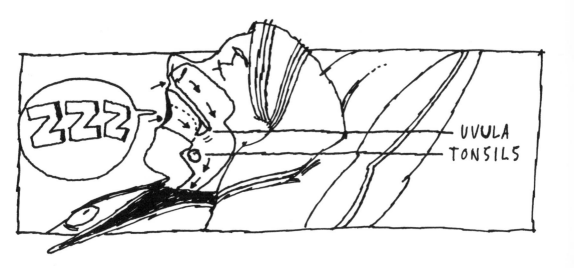

throat, the roof of your mouth is soft and flexible too. Even your lips and cheeks can be part of a snore.

When you sleep, all these parts of your body are loose and relaxed. Air makes some of these parts wiggle and flap back and forth as you breathe in or out. It's the flapping parts of you that make a snoring noise.

Some people snore whenever they sleep. Others only snore when their noses are stuffed up and they are forced to breathe through their mouths.

15

Every snorer has a different style. Some people sound like snorting horses; others sound like purring kittens. The sound of a snore depends on which parts are flapping or vibrating, how much air goes in and out of your mouth, and even what position you are lying in. The loudest snores usually come when you are lying on your back because more of your parts are relaxed and flapping.

Snores sound especially loud at night, because everything else is so quiet.

YAWNS

You yawn when you are tired. And when you are bored. When you are hungry. And when you are in a stuffy room. And often you yawn just because somebody near you has yawned.

Yawns are among the many body things that scientists can't explain. They really don't know what causes yawns, nor why they are so contagious. Sometimes even reading about yawning is enough to make you yawn.

When you are exercising, you hardly ever yawn. When you are angry or excited, you don't yawn either. Usually you have to be relaxed in order to yawn.

Probably some yawns happen because your body needs extra oxygen. A big yawn brings a lot of extra air—and oxygen—into your body. But certainly the need for oxygen doesn't explain why yawns are "catching."

Once a yawn starts, you can't stop it. If you close your mouth, the air will come in and go out through your nose, and your yawning muscles will still do the same yawning things. Yawning involves muscles in your face, in your throat, and in your cheeks.

Sometimes, yawns are accompanied by tears. That's because when you yawn, tiny muscles on the inside of your eyelids tighten up and squeeze tears into your eyes.

Yawns do not have to make any noise at all. You can yawn silently. But people often make noise when they yawn, just because they like to. If you want to know why a yawn makes noise, you'll have to ask the yawner.

HICCUPS

Everybody gets hiccups. But nobody understands them. Hiccups happen when something goes wrong with your diaphragm, the muscle between the chest and abdomen.

Your diaphragm helps you to breathe. When your diaphragm relaxes, it takes up so much room in your chest that it pushes the air out of your lungs. You breathe out.

When your diaphragm tightens, it be-

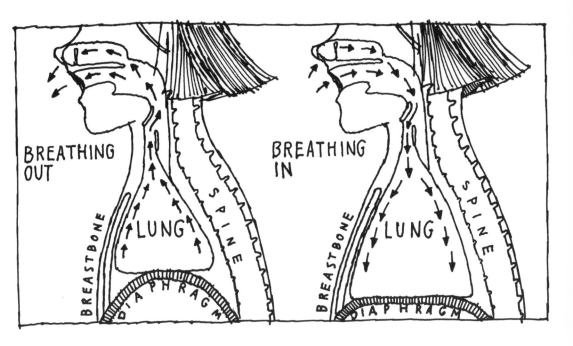

BREATHING OUT

BREATHING IN

BREASTBONE LUNG SPINE DIAPHRAGM

comes flat, like a plate, and leaves lots of space in your chest. You breathe in, and your lungs fill with air.

Your diaphragm starts working the minute you are born, and it never stops for your whole life. The diaphragm relaxes, the air goes out. The diaphragm tightens, the air goes in. Out and in. Out and in. No matter what you are doing, your diaphragm is always on the job.

But every once in a while—and nobody
knows why—your diaphragm gets mixed up.
Instead of sticking to its regular rhythm, it

24

jerks itself tight all of a sudden. That quick jerk is called a spasm.

When your diaphragm is tight, air is supposed to go in. But when the diaphragm spasms, something else interesting happens. For a fraction of a second, a tiny flap at the back of your throat called the epiglottis covers up the opening to your trachea, and no air can get down. When incoming air hits the epiglottis, you "hic."

1. The diaphragm spasms.

2. As the spasm occurs, air tries to get into your lungs.

3. The air bumps into the epiglottis. *Hic*.

For a little while after the *hic*, the diaphragm goes back to normal. But then it all happens again. The spasm. The air hitting the epiglottis. The *hic*.

Then your breathing returns to normal again. Soon another spasm. Air hits the epiglottis. *Hic.*

No one really knows where the spasms come from. They might come from swallowing food too quickly, or from a scare, or from laughing too hard.

The big question is how to get rid of hiccups. They usually stop by themselves. But they are annoying. Most people try to do things that they think will stop the hiccups right away.

Here are some of the things people do to try to get rid of hiccups. There are no guarantees that any of them will work.

1. Breathe deeply and slowly for five minutes.
2. Hold your breath as long as you can.
3. Put a paper bag over your nose and mouth; breathe into it for one or two minutes.

4. Have someone slap you across the back.
5. Get someone to scare you.
6. Drink a giant glass of water.
7. Put your hands above your head, hold your breath, and gulp down a glass of water (have someone else hold the glass).
8. Put a spoonful of peanut butter on the roof of your mouth and swallow it little by little.
9. Yank your tongue.

CRACKING BONES

Bodies sometimes make strange cracking noises. Wrists crack; knees crack; fingers, ankles, hips crack.

Actually, your bones don't really crack at all; they just make noises that sound like cracks. All the cracking noises have something to do with joints, the places where your bones come together.

There are two very different kinds of "cracking bones." One kind of crack happens when ligaments and tendons snap across your bones. The other kind happens when your bones pull away from each other with a sort of popping noise.

"SNAPPING" CRACKS

Your bones are held in place by ligaments— tough rubbery bands that look like tiny strips of tape. Ligaments attach your bones to each other. They attach your ankle bones to your leg bones and your leg bones to your knee bones, and your knee bones to your thigh bones. All the bones in your body stay where they belong because ligaments hold them in place.

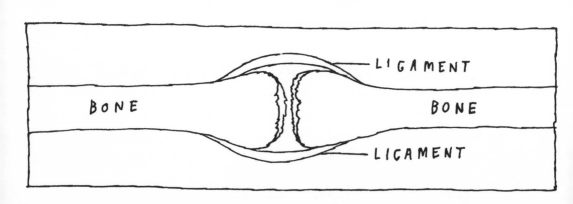

Tendons are made of the same stuff as ligaments. But unlike ligaments, which connect bones to bones, tendons connect muscles to bones. When the muscles pull on the tendons, your bones move—you walk, you eat, you brush your teeth.

Tendons and ligaments surround most of the joints in your body.

The end parts of bones are often bumpy. Sometimes, when you are moving around, tendons or ligaments (or both) snap across the bumps and make cracking sounds.

Ankles can crack. So can wrists and knees and shoulders and hips. Even jaws can crack when you open your mouth very wide. When tendons and ligaments snap, what happens

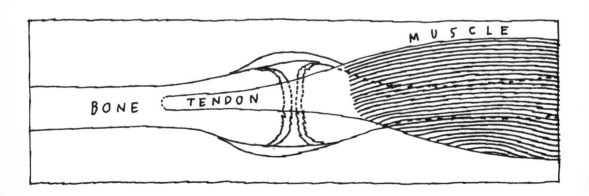

inside your body is very much like what happens when you snap your fingers. The noise in a finger snap is made when the snapped finger slides across the bump of your thumb and hits your hand. The snapping noise inside your body is made when tendons or ligaments skid across a bump and hit another part of you.

Some people "crack" more than others. Maybe their ligaments and tendons snap more easily. Or maybe their bones are bumpier.

"POPPING" CRACKS

Some people's knees crack when they do deep knee bends. Other people crack their knuckles on purpose, just to hear the noise.

The sound of cracking knuckles and knees can be very loud. You can often hear it across a big room. The loud cracking is the sound of a bubble bursting inside the knee or knuckle joint.

All the moving joints in your body are "oiled" with a gooey liquid called synovial fluid. The synovial fluid is always there, helping your bones to move smoothly. Synovial fluid cannot ooze out of your joints because it is held in by a fibrous covering that surrounds the joints.

There are tiny bubbles in the synovial fluid. They are so small that they can be seen only through a microscope.

Most of the time the bones of your joints press so tightly on the synovial fluid that the bubbles cannot get out; there is nowhere for them to go.

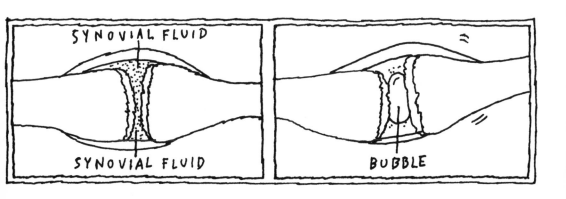

But sometimes when the bones are pulled away from each other, a space is created between them. The tiny bubbles come out of the synovial fluid into the space and clump together to form one bubble.

As the bones are pulled farther apart, the bubble gets bigger, until finally it bursts—and your bones "crack."

It is hard to imagine that such a little bubble can make such a big noise. But think about the loud cracking noises you can make with chewing gum.

After the synovial bubble has popped, it takes about twenty minutes for all the gas from the burst bubble to return to the synovial fluid as tiny bubbles. That's why knees will crack the first time someone does a deep knee bend, but not the second time. The same thing happens in the fingers. After someone cracks her or his knuckles, they won't crack again until the gas from the burst bubble has gone back into the synovial fluid.

Some people can't crack their knuckles and knees at all. That is probably because the strips of ligament that strap those people's bones together are short, and they won't stretch far enough to give the synovial bubble room to burst.

Luckily for those people, being able to crack knuckles and knees is of absolutely no use to the body. In fact, cracking your knuckles a lot might even be harmful. Doctors don't know for sure.

BURPS

Burps begin in your stomach. They start out as tiny bubbles sloshing around in the liquid mush that was once your food.

Most of the bubbles in your stomach are swallowed air. When you swallow chewed-up chicken, for example, lots of air goes down with the chicken. When you drink a glass of orange juice, you sometimes swallow more air than you do juice. Even your saliva is filled with bubbles of air.

You also swallow air or gases that are trapped in the drinks you drink and the foods you eat. Sodas are filled with bubbles. So are milk shakes and whipped cream. Even toast and popcorn are puffed with air. And an apple is packed with trapped gases that are set free by the acid juices in your stomach.

At first the bubbles of air swirl around in your stomach, all mixed up with the liquids. But eventually, like the bubbles in soda, many of the air bubbles in your stomach rise to the top of the liquid, and they pop.

As more and more bubbles pop, more and more air builds up in your stomach. The air presses against the inside of your stomach. When there is enough pressure, the air pushes its way up into your esophagus, the tube that leads from your stomach to your mouth. When the air reaches the top of the tube, it bursts out as a burp.

Some burps are noisy. Others are quiet.

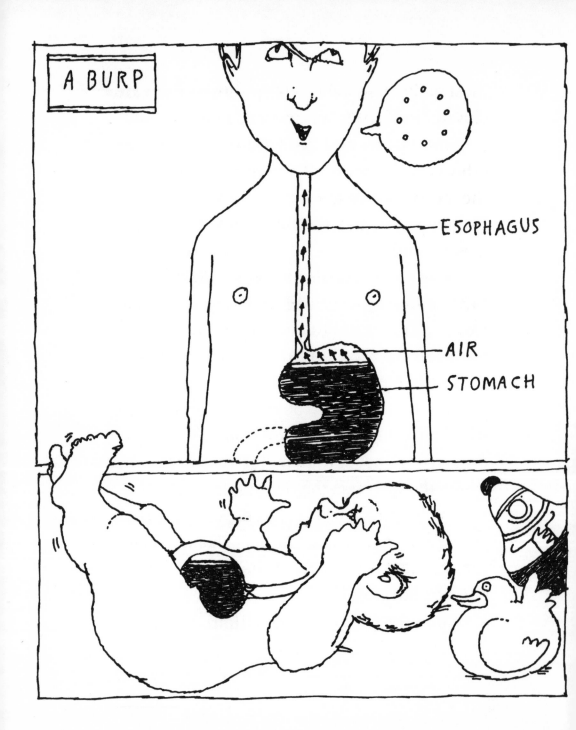

Most of the time you can burp with your mouth closed, and hardly anyone will notice.

Some foods and drinks are burpier than others. Soda, with all those gas bubbles, is the burpiest thing you can swallow. People usually burp just seconds after drinking a glass of soda.

Most people burp only when they have to. But some people can burp whenever they feel like making strange noises. A burp that someone makes on purpose usually comes from air that the person has sucked into the esophagus. Voluntary burps rarely come from stomach bubbles.

An interesting fact about burps is that when you lie on your back, the opening from your stomach into your esophagus is blocked by the liquid in your stomach. The air can't get out, so you can't burp. That's why babies have to be upright to be burped. If babies don't get burped, the air in their stomachs can't get out, and they feel uncomfortable.

The medical word for burping is "eructation," but not many people know or use that word. "Belch" is much more popular.

In some parts of the world, burps are embarrassing, and if you happen to burp in public, you have to say, "Excuse me."

In other parts of the world, a burp after a meal is a compliment to the cook.

And in still other places, if a hearty burp isn't given at the end of a meal as a sign of approval, the host is insulted.

STOMACH GROWLS

Your stomach is a powerful muscle. It squeezes and mashes and grinds your food into a pulpy, juicy mush. When your stomach has finished mashing up your meal, it pushes the mashed-up food into your intestines.

Your stomach is always working. It grinds and mashes and sloshes whatever is in there. But when you haven't eaten in a while, there's not much there—just a small amount of liquid and a lot of air. The liquid and the air splash and slosh around as your stomach

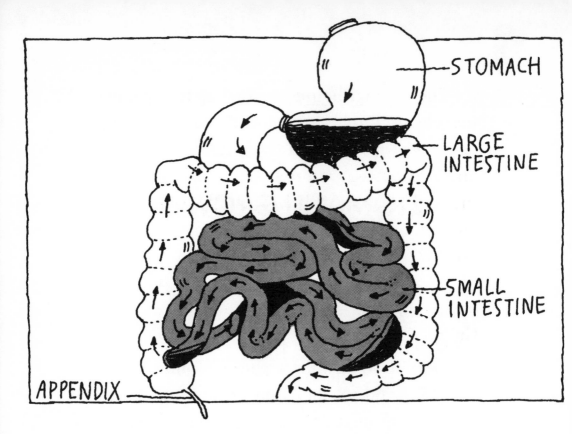

STOMACH

LARGE INTESTINE

SMALL INTESTINE

APPENDIX

grinds, and sometimes it sounds as though your stomach is growling.

Most of the time, the "stomach growls" you hear do not come from your stomach. They come from mashed-up, liquid food and air squeezing their way out of your stomach and squooshing through the long narrow twisty tubes of your intestines.

The air and liquid, pushed along by one muscle after another, squirt through narrow openings, up hills and down hills, and back and forth across your middle. All that squeezing and sloshing through small spaces creates a lot of noise. Most "growling stomachs" are really "growling intestines."

A lot of people think that growls happen only when you are hungry. They are wrong. Growls can happen anytime.

The scientific word for these noises is "borborygmi."

GAS

Some people say, "I expelled some gas." Others talk about "breaking wind." Doctors refer to "flatus" and "flatulence." And almost everyone knows about "farts."

They are noisy. They are smelly. They are embarrassing. They are also important. Everyone's body needs to get rid of the gases that build up in the digestive tract.

Your digestive tract, also called your gut, is a long, long tube that is all curled up inside of you. The tube has only two openings to the outside, one at each end. The opening at the top of the tube is your mouth; the opening at the bottom end is your anus—the hole through which you expel gas.

Everything you swallow moves through your digestive tract. Most of the food you eat is absorbed into your body as it moves through the intestines. But food isn't the only thing you swallow. With every chewed-up hunk of food, with every gulp of milk, with every swallow of saliva, you also swallow air.

The swallowed air goes right to your stomach. The air that doesn't come out as a burp moves on through your digestive tract. As it is pushed and squeezed through your intestines, it joins other clumps of swallowed air, and a bigger clump of air is formed.

Toward the end of the digestive tract, other gases are added to the swallowed air. The new gases are created when tiny living things called bacteria attack bits of food. There are always bacteria in your digestive tract. They help your body digest certain foods, such as the strings from celery, the skin of corn kernels, the outside covering of beans.

When a clump of air finally reaches the end of the digestive tract, it bumps into an almost solid wall. The exit is held tightly closed by a muscle called the anal sphincter.

As the air sits there, more air and gas join it. Pressure builds as the clump of air gets larger and pushes on the anal sphincter.

Sometimes the pressure builds up so much that you can't control your anal sphincter. The gas just bursts out. There is the same kind of blast when you puff up your cheeks and then, with your lips tightly closed, force the air out by pushing on your cheeks.

Other times, you can tighten your anal sphincter so that the gas won't come out at an embarrassing time or place.

But if you want to, you can help to force

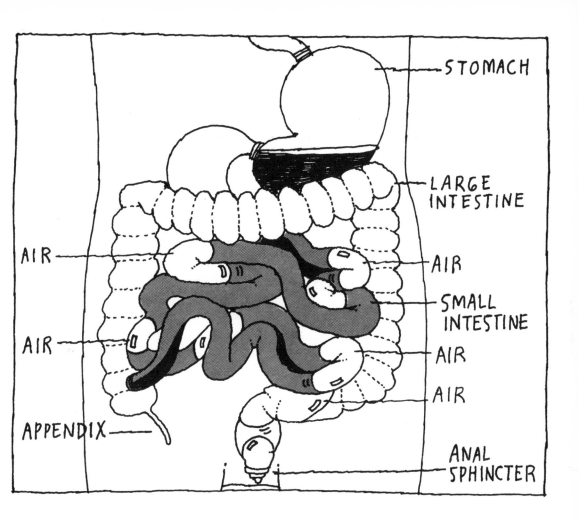

STOMACH

LARGE INTESTINE

AIR

AIR

AIR

SMALL INTESTINE

AIR

AIR

APPENDIX

ANAL SPHINCTER

the gas out by relaxing your anal sphincter, tightening other muscles, and "pushing" out the gas.

The tightness or looseness of the anal

49

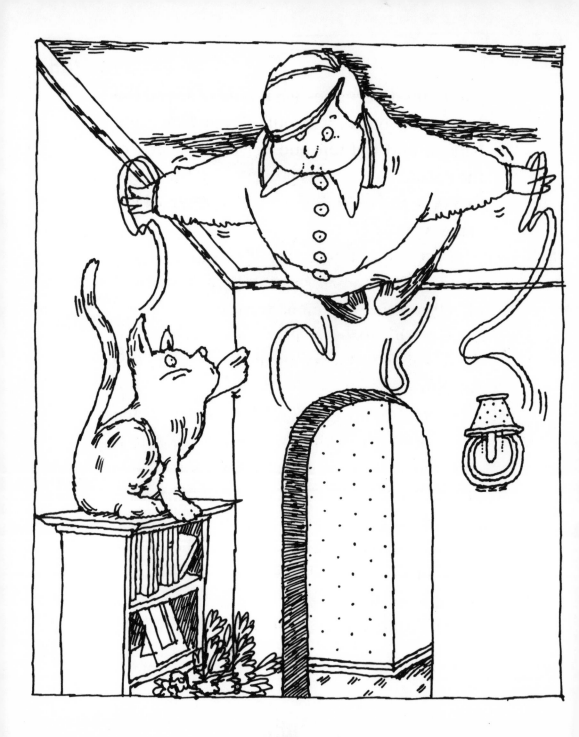

sphincter determines what kind of sound the gas makes on its way out. If you blow up a balloon and tighten and loosen the neck of the balloon as the air is pushing out, the sound made by the escaping air will change in the same way.

Everybody knows that all gas is not the same. Sometimes it has hardly any smell at all. Other times it smells terrible.

The bad-smelling gas usually comes when bacteria have attacked foods that have a lot of sulphur in them.

Sulphur is an awful-smelling chemical. You can't smell the sulphur when it is in your food; but when the tiny bacteria attack bits of sulphur-containing food in the digestive tract, they turn the sulphur into a smelly gas. Onions, cabbage, cauliflower, and beans are some of the foods that produce the most—and the smelliest—gas.

It is a combination of the smell and the

noise that makes people feel so embarrassed when they expel gas. One thing is certain— everybody does it. One medical report says that the normal adult male expels gas about ten to eighteen times a day.

A second thing that is certain is that people have different ways of talking about expelling gas. They may call it "breaking wind," "passing gas," "cutting the cheese," or "laying one."

There are plenty of other names, too: gasser, breezer, fart, fizz, cheeser, whiffle, poop, SBD (silent-but-deadly), and low-flying duck. You can probably add some of your own to the list.

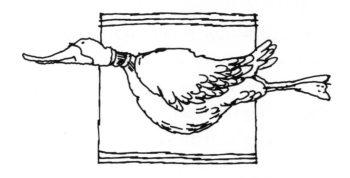

A FINAL WORD
ABOUT BODY NOISES

Understanding how and why body noises happen may not make them less embarrassing, but it certainly will give you something to think and talk about.

Now you can follow your burps up the esophagus and your gassy growls through your intestines. And whenever you hear someone

53

snoring, you will probably get a picture in your head of all those mouth and throat parts flapping around.

You probably know more about body noises than your friends, your parents, and your teachers. And you are one of only a few thousand people in the world who know about synovial bubbles.

Congratulations!

SUSAN KOVACS BUXBAUM was born and raised in Pough-keepsie, New York. She attended Mount Holyoke College and New York University Graduate School of Biology and worked for several years as a medical researcher. In a switch from biological science to political science, she now works for the political unit at ABC News. Susan lives in New York City with her husband. They have two children.

RITA GOLDEN GELMAN grew up in Bridgeport, Connecticut. After graduating from Brandeis University, she took a job as a file clerk for a children's magazine. "I messed up the files so badly that they promoted me to staff writer—just to keep me away from the file drawers," she says. Since then, she has written more than forty children's books. Rita is currently working on a Ph.D. in anthropology at U.C.L.A. She lives in Los Angeles with her husband. Both of their children are published authors.

Susan and Rita met when their children attended the same nursery school. They have collaborated on two previous books. *Body Noises* is their first book for Knopf.

ANGIE LLOYD received a BFA degree with honors from the Rhode Island School of Design and has studied at the Parsons School of Design. As a child she started illustrating by coloring in the black and white line drawings in several of her books, and she has never stopped. Her work has appeared in two textbooks and on the editorial page of *The New York Times*. Ms. Lloyd and her husband live in New York City.